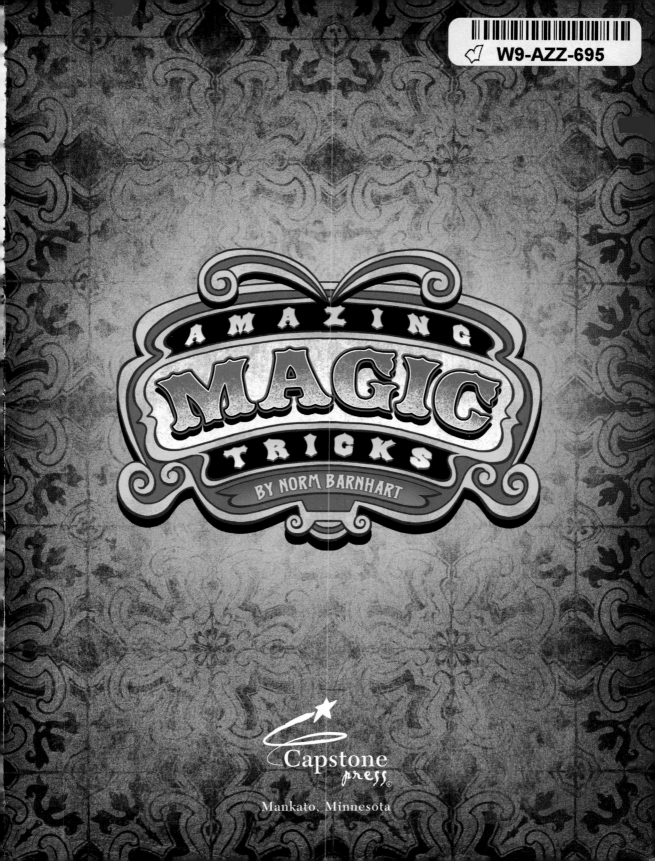

AMAZING MAGIC TRICKS

BY NORM BARNHART

Capstone press®

Mankato, Minnesota

TABLE OF CONTENTS

WELCOME TO MAGIC!

Have you ever wondered how magicians do their incredible tricks? How do they make things appear or disappear? Can they really read people's minds? With this book, you'll discover some of the secrets magicians don't want you to know. Grab your magic wand and take a peek behind the curtain to learn some amazing magic!

THE KEYS TO MAGIC

➜ Practice, practice, practice! If you want your tricks to work right, you need to practice until you can do them quickly and smoothly. Try standing in front of a mirror while practicing. Then you can see what the tricks will look like to your audience.

➜ Keep it secret! Magicians never share their secrets. If you reveal the secrets of a trick, people won't be very impressed. It also ruins the trick for other magicians who want to do it in the future.

➜ Be entertaining! Try telling the audience some jokes or stories that relate to your tricks while performing them. Keep the audience entertained, and they won't notice how the tricks are done. It will also keep them coming back for more.

BEFORE YOU BEGIN

Most magicians hide their props in a magic box. A magic box will help you keep your tricks organized and your special props hidden from the audience. You can make your own magic box. Find a cardboard box and decorate it with some colorful stars, or cover it with dark cloth so it looks mysterious.

A magic wand is a magician's most useful tool. Wands help direct people's attention to what you want them to see. You can make a wand out of a wooden dowel painted black and white. Or roll up a piece of black construction paper and tape the ends. You can add sparkles and stars if you wish. Be creative and have fun!

CHAPTER 1
BEGINNER
LEVEL

BEWILDERING!

BREATHTAKING!

AMAZING MAGIC!

You don't need to be a master magician to perform magic. In this chapter, you'll learn simple, fun tricks that will astound your audience. You can make objects magically appear or disappear right before their eyes! It's easy when you know the secrets behind the tricks.

A MAGIC SECRET - PALMING

Magicians often use a method called palming to make things seem to vanish out of thin air. To do it, they secretly hide objects in the palm of their hand. Try practicing this method in front of a mirror so your hand looks natural. Once you learn to palm objects, you can amaze your friends with your magical abilities!

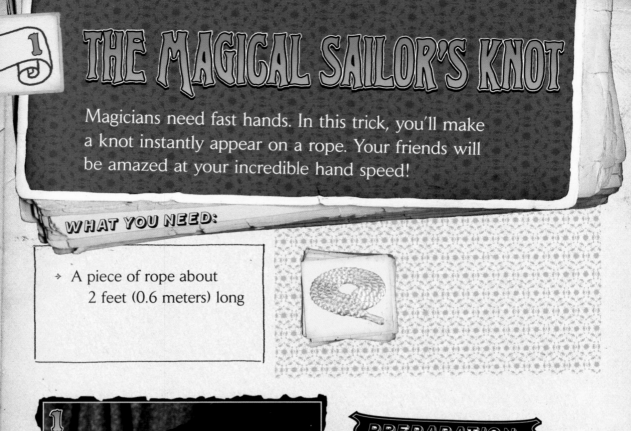

THE MAGICAL SAILOR'S KNOT

Magicians need fast hands. In this trick, you'll make a knot instantly appear on a rope. Your friends will be amazed at your incredible hand speed!

WHAT YOU NEED:

→ A piece of rope about 2 feet (0.6 meters) long

PREPARATION:

1. Tie a large knot in one end of the rope as shown.

PERFORMANCE:

2. First, show the audience the rope. Hold it with the knot secretly hidden in your hand as shown.

Hidden knot

3. Now hold the other end of the rope between your thumb and first finger as shown. Be sure to keep the knot hidden. Tell the audience that your hands are faster than the eye, and that you can make a knot appear out of thin air.

4. With your free hand, pretend to grab an invisible knot out of the air. Then toss it at the rope.

As you toss the invisible knot, let go of the untied end. Say, "Oops, I missed. I'll try again."

5. Hold the untied end up like before. Pretend to throw the invisible knot again and drop the untied end. Say, "Wow, I missed again." Act a bit disappointed and then try a third time.

The third time it will work. This time let go of the end with the knot. The knot magically appears on the rope!

magic tip: By failing at first, the audience will be more amazed when you make the knot seem to magically appear.

TRICKY TREATS

Everybody loves candy. Wouldn't it be great if you could make candy appear out of nowhere? You can do just that with this quick and easy hanky trick.

WHAT YOU NEED:

→ A colorful handkerchief
→ A piece of wrapped candy

PREPARATION:

1. Hold the candy between your thumb and fingers as shown. It's best to use wrapped candy so your hand doesn't get sticky.

2. Next, hold the hanky in the fingers of the same hand so the candy is hidden. The audience will think you're only holding the hanky.

3. Wave the hanky in the air and act as if it's empty. Nobody should suspect that you're hiding the candy in that hand. Then place the hanky over the palm of your empty hand as shown.

4. Next, drag the hanky across your open hand. Show the audience that your hand is empty. This step helps people believe there is nothing there.

5. Now pull the hanky across your hand again. This time, drop the candy into your open hand. The candy magically appears! Give the candy to someone in the audience to enjoy during the show.

FIND THE MAGIC RABBIT

Lots of magicians like pulling rabbits out of their hats. But there's more than one way to find a magic rabbit. In this trick, a magical paper bunny is the star of the show!

WHAT YOU NEED:

- → A marker or crayon
- → A colorful handkerchief
- → A sheet of paper

PREPARATION:

1. Draw a carrot, a bunny, and a hat on the paper as shown. Make sure the bunny is in the middle section. Leave plenty of space between each picture.

PERFORMANCE:

2. First, show the audience the paper with the three pictures. Then fold the paper between the pictures and tear it into three pieces along the folds.

3. Next, turn the pictures upside down. Ask a volunteer to mix up the pictures and cover them with the hanky while your back is turned.

4. When the volunteer is finished, turn back to the table. With a mysterious look on your face say, "I can find the bunny without looking under the hanky." Then reach under the hanky to get the rabbit.

5. Now pull out the picture of the rabbit and take a bow! The secret to this trick is easy. When you reach under the hanky, simply feel the sides of each piece of paper. Since the rabbit is drawn on the center piece, it is the only paper with two torn sides. It's a simple trick that will keep your friends guessing how it's done!

Torn sides

magic tip: Try this trick with some different drawings. You could draw the faces of two boys and a girl, or two dogs and a cat.

JACK, THE INCREDIBLE CARD

That Jack of Diamonds is one strong card. This super stunt will amaze your friends. They'll watch in wonder as Jack balances a cup on his top edge!

WHAT YOU NEED:

→ One Jack of Diamonds card
→ One other card
→ A foam cup
→ Tape
→ Scissors

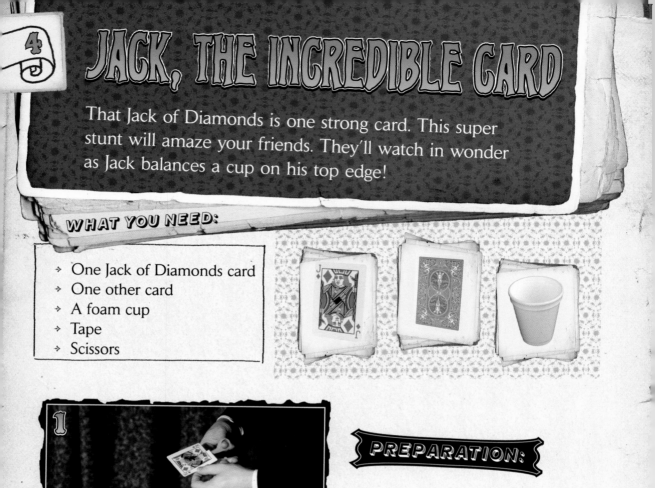

PREPARATION:

1. First, cut the extra card in half lengthwise as shown.

2. Next, tape one half of the cut card to the back of the Jack of Diamonds as shown. This creates a secret flap. When the flap is down, the back of the Jack should look like a normal card.

3. Hold up the cup and the Jack card. Show the audience both sides of the card and say, "Jack looks like a normal card, but he's really strong. He can do an amazing balancing act."

4. Now place the cup on the edge of the card. Secretly bring out the flap to balance the cup as shown.

5. Finally, pull your hand away to show that the Jack card is balancing the cup. Ask the audience to give Jack a round of applause and have him take a bow!

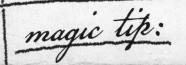

magic tip: Always keep the back of the card toward you when the flap is out. Otherwise the secret of the trick will be revealed.

WONDERFUL APPEARING WAND

Every magician needs a magic wand. This trick will astound your audience as your magic wand appears in an impossible way.

WHAT YOU NEED:

→ A magic wand
→ A large box of candy
→ A jacket or shirt with long sleeves
→ Scissors

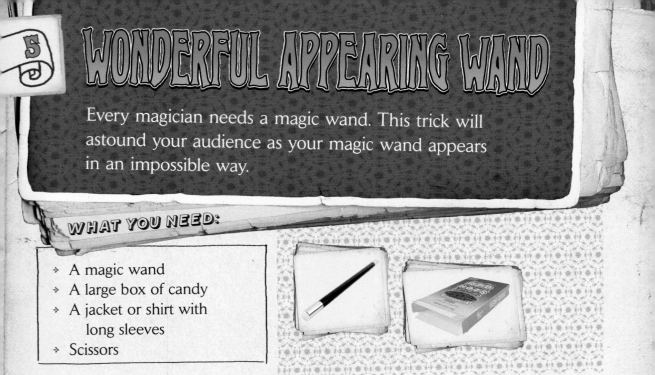

PREPARATION:

1. First, take the candy out of the box and save some for later. Then cut a small hole in the bottom of the box. Make sure the hole is a little larger than your magic wand.

2. Next, slide the wand up your sleeve as shown. When you're ready to do the trick, you'll simply slide the wand through the hole in the box. Put the candy you saved back in the box.

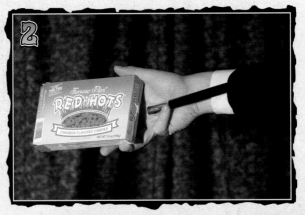

Secret hole

3. First, reach into your magic box for the candy box. While your hands are hidden, slide the end of the wand through the secret hole. Then show the candy box to your audience. Say, "I like this candy. One in every ten thousand boxes has a special gift!" Be sure to keep the secret hole hidden in your hand.

4. Now start eating some of the candy from the box. As you eat, pretend that you find something inside. Act surprised, then reach in and start pulling out the magic wand.

5. Finally, pull the wand out of the box and show it to the audience. Say, "Wow, this is my lucky day!" Now you have a magic wand to help you perform the rest of your show!

INVISIBLE MAGIC GLUE

Your friends will wonder how your wand sticks to your fingers with this mysterious trick. They'll be amazed when the wand falls off with a snap of their fingers!

WHAT YOU NEED:

> A magic wand
> A small empty bottle

PERFORMANCE:

1. Any small bottle will work for this trick. Start by telling your audience that the bottle holds invisible magic glue.

Next, hold your wand in one hand and pretend to pour the glue all over the wand and your fingers.

magic tip: Try using your acting skills to add humor to this trick. Pretend that the wand won't come off, no matter how hard you shake your hand!

2. Close your hand around the wand and put the bottle back in your magic box.

Now grip your wrist with your other hand and slide your finger up to hold the wand as shown. Don't let your friends see your finger or the trick will be ruined!

3. Next, slowly open your hand to show that the wand is stuck in place. Say, "This invisible glue is some really sticky stuff!"

4. When you want the glue to disappear, just ask a friend to snap his or her fingers. At that moment, let the wand go by moving your finger. The wand is no longer stuck to your hand!

AMAZING APPEARING BALL

"Where did that ball come from?" That's what your friends will ask when you make this ball magically appear from an empty cup!

WHAT YOU NEED:

→ A ping-pong ball
→ A foam cup
→ A magic wand

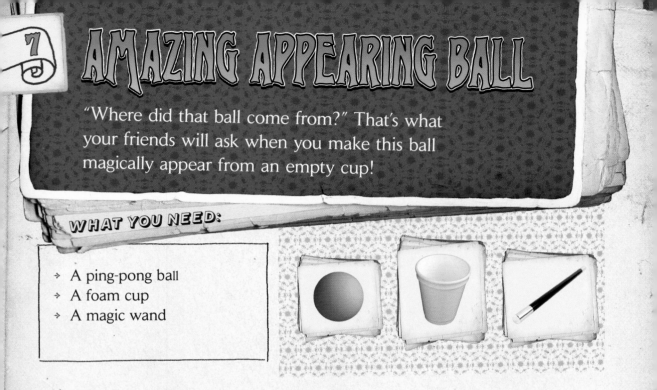

PREPARATION:

1. First, poke a hole in the foam cup so your finger can slip into it.

Now place the ball in the cup and use your third finger to hold it in place as shown.

magic tip: Add some fun to this trick by drawing a face on the ball and giving it a fun name. Pretend that it likes to play hide-and-seek!

2. First tip over the cup to show that it's empty. Then tell the audience, "Things aren't always how they appear. This cup might look empty, but it's not." Be sure not to let anyone see the ball or your finger inside the cup!

3. Now hold the cup high and wave your magic wand over it. While you do this, you can say a few made-up magic words.

4. Finally, tip over the cup and let the ball fall into your open hand. The ball magically appears!

Show the audience the ball and toss it to someone. While they're looking at it, drop the special cup into your magic box. Nobody will ever know the secret!

THE FANTASTIC FLOWER

Flowers grow quickly in the spring. But with this trick, you can make a flower appear instantly with special magic seeds. Your friends will be really impressed!

WHAT YOU NEED:

→ A small flower pot
→ A fake flower
→ An empty seed packet
→ A magic wand

PREPARATION:

1. Place the flower in the flower pot. Then put the pot in your magic box.

PERFORMANCE:

2. When you're ready to do this trick, hide the flower by holding it against the side of the pot as shown.

Hidden flower

3. Hold up the pot so the audience can see that it's empty. Be sure to keep the flower hidden under your hand.

4. Tell the audience about your magic flower seeds. Say, "These are the world's fastest growing flowers." Pretend to sprinkle some invisible seeds from the seed packet into the flower pot.

Next, wave your magic wand over the pot and say a few magic words.

5. Now reach in and pull out the pretty flower that has magically grown inside! You can give the flower to your mom or a friend as a gift.

THE MYSTERIOUS CAR TRICK

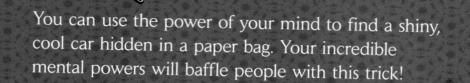

You can use the power of your mind to find a shiny, cool car hidden in a paper bag. Your incredible mental powers will baffle people with this trick!

WHAT YOU NEED:

→ Three small paper bags
→ One shiny cool toy car
→ Two dull toy cars
→ A pencil

PREPARATION:

1. Place a small, secret pencil mark in the lower right corner of one bag as shown. Don't make the mark too dark or someone might see it and learn how this trick works.

PERFORMANCE:

2. First, show the three cars to the audience. Place the shiny cool car in the marked bag. Place the dull cars in the other bags. Then fold over the tops of all three bags. Keep the secret mark facing you so nobody sees it.

Secret mark

3. Tell the audience about your amazing mental powers. Say, "I can use my mind to find the cool car, even if the bags are mixed up." Then turn around and ask a volunteer from the audience to mix up the bags.

4. Now turn back to the table and pretend to use your mind powers to find the cool car. Hold up each bag and look at it closely. Pretend to concentrate hard on what's inside. While doing this, you will really be looking for the bag with the secret mark.

5. When you find the marked bag say, "This is it! I've found the cool car." Reach in and pull out the cool car. Take a bow as the audience applauds your amazing mental powers!

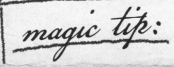 Try acting like you don't know which bag is correct at first. The audience will be even more amazed when you find the cool car!

ZARCON, THE INVISIBLE HERO

The alien hero Zarcon has worked hard to bring criminals to justice. Now it's time for him to go home. With a wave of your magic wand, he disappears and travels back to his own planet.

WHAT YOU NEED:

→ A colorful handkerchief
→ A small action figure
→ A secret helper
→ A magic wand

PERFORMANCE:

1. Show Zarcon to the audience and tell them he wants to return to his home planet. Tell them that you're going to help him with a bit of magic. When you're ready for the trick, hold the toy in your hand as shown.

2. Next, place the hanky over your hand to hide Zarcon as shown.

3. Now ask two volunteers to feel under the hanky to make sure Zarcon hasn't disappeared yet.

4. The second person will really be your secret helper. Your helper will secretly take Zarcon from your hand as shown, and then hide the toy in his or her pocket. Ask your secret helper, "Is Zarcon still there?" He or she should say, "Yes."

5. After your helper takes Zarcon, wave your magic wand over the hanky. Finally, remove the hanky and show the audience that Zarcon has disappeared!

magic tip: Be sure to practice this trick with your helper ahead of time. Make it look smooth and natural and the audience won't suspect a thing.

FAST RABBIT AND THE ACE

People love card tricks. They love to watch cards magically switch locations or change colors. In this trick, your magic rabbit loves the Ace of Diamonds so much he can't resist stealing it!

WHAT YOU NEED:

→ A deck of cards
→ A small stuffed bunny
→ A table

PREPARATION:

1. First, separate the four aces from the deck of cards. Place the Ace of Diamonds on top of the deck of cards. Then set the other three aces on top of the Ace of Diamonds.

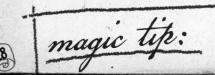

magic tip: If you don't have a bunny, you can use any other small stuffed toy for this trick.

2. Introduce your stuffed bunny to the audience. Tell them he really loves the Ace of Diamonds. Say that he sometimes steals it so fast that you can't even see him move!

Take the three aces from the top of the deck and set them aside. Be sure to leave the Ace of Diamonds on top of the deck. Then place the bunny on top of the deck.

3. Arrange the three aces with the Ace of Hearts in the middle as shown. Hold the cards close together so the Ace of Hearts looks like the Ace of Diamonds as shown in the second picture above. Then ask a volunteer to help with this trick. Show the volunteer the aces. Ask if he or she sees the Ace of Diamonds. The volunteer should say, "Yes."

TURN PAGE FOR MORE!

4. Next, lay the aces one by one face down on the table. Make sure the volunteer doesn't see the front of the cards. Ask the volunteer to guess which card is the Ace of Diamonds. He or she will probably pick the middle card.

5. Flip the card over to show that it is really the Ace of Hearts. Your volunteer will probably be surprised! Ask the volunteer to try picking a different card.

6. Flip over the next chosen card. It won't be the Ace of Diamonds either. Do this again with the third card so all three aces are face up.

7. It's time to show where the Ace of Diamonds went. Say, "Look at that — the Ace of Diamonds is gone! I bet my magic bunny ran over and stole it so fast that we couldn't see it."

Lift the bunny off the deck of cards. Pick up the top card and show that he's been sitting on the Ace of Diamonds! Thank your volunteer and have the bunny take a bow.

CHAPTER 2
APPRENTICE
LEVEL

ASTOUNDING!

ASTONISHING!

MYSTERIOUS MAGIC!

Magicians have performed mysterious mental magic for hundreds of years. They have rarely shared their secrets with anyone. In this chapter, you'll learn some more complex magic secrets, including some mind-bending mental tricks. Are you ready to astound audiences with your mysterious mental powers? I knew you would be!

A MAGIC SECRET - ASSISTANTS

Magicians often need assistants to help them perform their tricks. Most assistants are really secret helpers who know the secrets behind the tricks. Sometimes they sit in the crowd and pretend to be part of the audience. Assistants help the magician make the tricks look real. Find a good secret assistant, and you'll have lots of fun fooling people with your magic tricks.

THE MAGIC ROBOT

Some robots seem to have magical abilities. In this trick, the audience will gasp when they see a toy robot magically move from your pocket back to its box.

WHAT YOU NEED:

→ Two identical toy robots
→ A small box

PREPARATION:

1. First, cut a hole in the back of the box as shown. Be sure the hole is large enough to fit your finger. Then place both robots into the box.

PERFORMANCE:

2. Start by picking up the box and holding one of the toy robots with your finger as shown. Tip over the box and drop the other robot into your hand. Don't let the audience see that you're holding the secret robot inside the box.

3. Next, show the audience the robot and tell them a story about how it can perform an amazing magic act. Explain how it can move so fast that they won't even see it move. Then place the robot in your pocket.

4. Hold up the box and wave your magic wand over it. You can say some made-up magic words to help fool the audience. Or you can pretend that you feel something jump out of your pocket.

5. Finally, tip over the box and drop the hidden robot into your hand. Show it to the audience and have it take a bow!

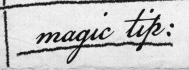

magic tip: Be sure to keep the hole in the box hidden from the audience. If they see it, they'll learn the secret of the trick.

AMAZING SPORTS PREDICTION

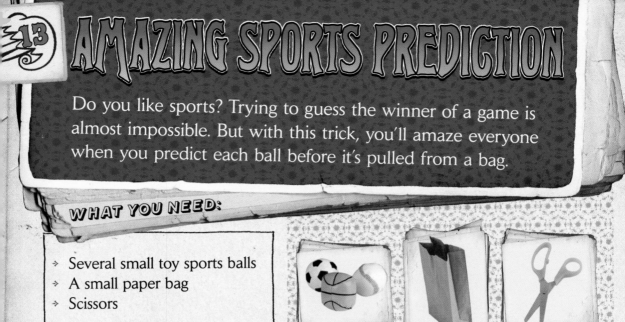

Do you like sports? Trying to guess the winner of a game is almost impossible. But with this trick, you'll amaze everyone when you predict each ball before it's pulled from a bag.

WHAT YOU NEED:

→ Several small toy sports balls
→ A small paper bag
→ Scissors

PREPARATION:

1. First, cut a small hole in the bottom back corner of the paper bag as shown.

2. Then fold the bag back again so the hole is hidden.

3. First, tell the audience about your amazing predictions. Tell them you can guess which ball will be pulled out of the bag.

Pick up the bag and unfold it, making sure to keep the hole hidden. Pinch the hole closed so nobody sees it, then show the audience that the bag is empty.

4. Now ask a volunteer to drop the balls into the bag. Then hold the bag by the front upper corner as shown. Be sure to hold the bag so the secret hole faces you. The balls will roll to the rear. You should be able to see a bit of one ball through the secret hole. If you see the baseball say, "I predict that the baseball will be picked first."

Secret hole

5. Finally, close your eyes and reach into the bag. Go to the back corner, pull out the baseball, and show it to the audience. Do this twice more, announcing which ball will be picked each time. When the balls are gone, crumple up the bag and toss it in your magic box. Everyone will wonder how you made your amazing predictions!

THE PHOENIX BALLOON

Is it possible to put a popped balloon back together again? It is with this fun trick. The audience will be stunned when they see a popped balloon magically made whole again.

WHAT YOU NEED:

→ Two identical balloons
→ A large paper bag
→ A fork

PREPARATION:

1. First, blow up one balloon and tie it. Then place it at the bottom of the paper bag as shown. Place the empty balloon in the bag so it can be dumped out easily.

PERFORMANCE:

2. Start by telling the audience about your magic balloon. Say, "This balloon can restore itself if it's popped!" Then tip over the bag so the empty balloon drops onto the table. Don't let the secret filled balloon fall out.

3. Next, blow up the empty balloon, tie it, and show it to the audience. Then pop it with the fork and place the pieces back into the bag. You can have fun by saying something like, "This looks bad. I don't know if the balloon can fix itself this time!"

4. Now close the top of the bag and wave your magic wand over it. You can say a few made-up magic words too.

5. Finally, open up the bag and pull out the filled balloon. The audience will think the balloon magically restored itself. Take a bow as they applaud!

magic tip: Try adding some fun to this trick. Pretend that the balloon pieces are jumping around in the bag as they try to join together again.

THE AMAZING BRAIN-E-O

Use the power of your brain to read people's minds! Your friends will be amazed as you tell them what objects they are thinking about. It's easy when you know the secret.

WHAT YOU NEED:

→ Ten random objects
→ A secret assistant

PERFORMANCE:

1. Start this trick by telling the audience about your amazing mind-reading powers. Tell them you can read their minds and that you can prove it. Ask your secret assistant to help with this trick. Then turn your back to the audience.

2. While your back is turned, your assistant asks a volunteer to choose an object on the table. The volunteer should not say the object's name out loud. Instead, the volunteer should just point at the chosen object.

3. Before doing this trick, you should arrange to have your assistant point at the chosen object on the third try. Now turn back to the table. Your assistant should point to a different object and ask if it is the chosen item. You'll say, "No, that's not correct."

4. Your assistant then points at a second item on the table. Concentrate hard on that object and act as if you aren't sure if it's correct. Finally, you'll say, "No that's not the right one either."

5. On the third try, your assistant will point at the correct object. Now act like the trick has become really easy and say, "Yes, that's it!" The audience will be stunned by your amazing mind-reading powers!

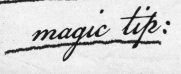

magic tip: Try this trick again, but this time the chosen item will be the fifth one your assistant points to. The audience will wonder how you can read their minds!

THE PUZZLING PUZZLE

You can use your mind powers to do more than just guess what people are thinking. You will really leave your audience puzzled with this mind-bending puzzle trick!

WHAT YOU NEED:

→ Two small, identical puzzles
→ Two small paper bags
→ Scissors
→ Tape

PREPARATION:

1. First, cut one bag in half lengthwise as shown. Be sure to leave the bottom of the bag attached.

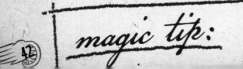

magic tip: Use some glue or tape on the back of the hidden puzzle to hold it together while it's inside the secret pocket.

2. Then place the cut bag inside the whole bag. Tape the sides to hold it in place. This creates a secret pocket on one side where you can hide a puzzle.

3. Next, assemble one of the puzzles, but leave one piece out. Then slide the puzzle into the secret pocket as shown.

PERFORMANCE:

4. First, tell the audience about your mysterious mind powers. Say, "Puzzles are fun, but they take too long to put together. I like using my mind instead." Then tip the bag over to show the audience that it's empty. As you tip it, hold the secret pocket closed as shown.

TURN PAGE FOR MORE!

5. Next, drop the puzzle pieces into the bag. Leave one puzzle piece on the table. This piece should match the one you left out before. You can mark the back of it to remember which piece it is.

6. Now shake the bag gently. Pretend that you're concentrating hard to put the puzzle together with the power of your mind.

7. Slowly pull the hidden puzzle out of the secret pocket. Be sure the audience can see that the puzzle is fully assembled, except for one missing piece. Then toss the bag into your magic box.

8. Finally, pick up the extra puzzle piece and place it into the puzzle. Leaving one piece out helps the audience believe that you really assembled the puzzle with your mind. Take a bow while the audience applauds your mysterious mind powers!

IT'S PARTY TIME!

Celebrate the New Year, a friend's birthday, or any special occasion with this fun, flashy trick. You'll be the life of the party when you make a shower of confetti instantly appear.

WHAT YOU NEED:

→ Two identical file folders
→ A sheet of colorful paper
→ A marker
→ Scissors
→ Glue

PREPARATION:

1. First, cut 1 inch (2.5 centimeters) off the top of one folder. Then glue one side of the short folder inside the other folder as shown.

2. Next, cut the sheet of paper in half. Using the marker, write a message like "Happy New Year!" on both halves of the paper. Then cut one half of the paper into confetti. Place it in one of the open sections inside the folder as shown.

3. Tell the audience, "It's time for a party!" Then show them the empty section of the folder.

Next, show the audience the uncut paper with the message written on it. Then place it into the empty section of the folder.

4. Now it's time for the magic. Concentrate hard on the folder and say a few magic words. Pretend that you're cutting up the paper inside with magic invisible scissors as shown.

5. Finally, pop open the folder so a shower of confetti fills the air! Be sure to keep the uncut paper hidden inside the closed section of the folder. Put the folder in your magic box and take a bow!

magic tip: Make sure none of the confetti falls out when you show the empty folder to the audience. If they see it, they'll know you cheated!

THE FREAKY MIND WELD

Paper clips are easy to lose. It's easier to keep track of them if they're linked together. This trick will astonished your audience when they see your magic mind powers at work!

WHAT YOU NEED:

- → 20 paper clips
- → An envelope
- → Glue

PREPARATION:

Glue here.

1. First, link ten paper clips and place them in the corner of the envelope. Next, glue the inside of the envelope as shown to make a secret pocket. The linked clips will be sealed inside. Then put the ten loose clips into the open part of the envelope.

PERFORMANCE:

2. Show the envelope to the audience and say, "I found an easy way to keep paper clips together." Open the envelope and pour out the loose clips.

3. Tell the audience, "All I have to do is link the clips together with my mind." Put the clips back in the envelope, one at a time. Count out loud as you do this so the audience knows how many paper clips there are. Then lick the envelope and seal it.

4. Now hold the envelope up to your forehead. Pretend to use your powerful mental energy to link the paper clips together. Pretending to concentrate hard makes this trick seem really mysterious for the audience.

5. Now rip open the end of the envelope with the secret pocket. Grab the end of the linked clips and slowly pull them out. The audience will be astonished when they see that the clips are linked together. You have one powerful brain!

magic tip: Try attaching a small toy soldier to the end of the paper clip chain. Then pretend to be surprised when you find that the soldier did all the work!

MESSAGE FROM A GHOST

You can freak out your friends with this spooky trick. When your pet ghost sends you a creepy message, they'll be too scared to move!

WHAT YOU NEED:

→ A shoebox
→ Two sheets of paper
→ A marker

PREPARATION:

1. Write a creepy message like "Boo!" on one sheet of paper. Crumple the message into a ball. Then place it into the shoebox with the blank sheet of paper. Keep the marker and cover of the shoebox in your magic box.

PERFORMANCE:

2. Tell your friends you have a pet ghost and that it likes to leave you messages. Get out the shoebox and take out the blank sheet of paper. At the same time, secretly hide the crumpled ball in your hand as shown.

Message

Message

Blank paper

3. Show that the paper is blank on both sides, then crumple it into a ball. As you crumple it, secretly switch it with the paper hidden in your hand. Then drop the message into the shoebox. Be sure to keep the blank paper hidden in your hand.

4. Next, get the marker and shoebox cover out of your magic box. When you reach in, drop the blank paper. Toss the marker into the shoebox and put on the cover. Then shake the box and pretend to wrestle with it as if your pet ghost was moving around inside.

5. Finally, remove the shoebox cover and take out the paper. Ask someone to open it and read it. Your friends will be amazed at the spooky message that has appeared!

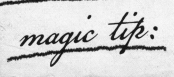

magic tip: Before doing this trick, try telling the audience a story about the ghost. Maybe you trapped it by the light of the full moon. Or maybe it's a friendly ghost that likes to help out with your magic show!

20

WHERE'S ROVER?

Mental magic can help you read people's minds, make predictions, or put a puzzle together. And with this astounding trick, it can even help you find a lost dog!

WHAT YOU NEED:

→ Three cups
→ A small toy dog
→ A secret assistant
→ A table

1. First, show the toy dog and the cups to the audience, then set the props on the table. Tell the audience you have a special mental connection with the dog. Say, "Rover is my special pal. I can find him even if he gets lost under the cups."

2. Next, ask your secret assistant, who is sitting in the audience, to come and help you with this trick. Then turn your back to the table. Ask your secret assistant to place the toy dog under one of the cups and mix them up.

3. Turn back to the table when your assistant is done. Then begin pretending to use your mental powers to see which cup the dog is under.

You will be able to find the correct cup by looking at your secret assistant's feet.

4. If the dog is under the left cup, your assistant's foot will point to the left.

If the dog is under the center cup, your assistant's feet both point forward.

If the dog is under the right cup, your assistant's foot will point to the right.

5. Once you know where the toy dog is, lift up the cup to reveal the toy. The audience will be stunned by your awesome mental powers!

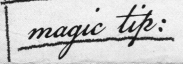
magic tip: Be sure to practice this trick with your secret assistant before performing it. If he or she acts cool and calm, everything should go smoothly.

21

RICKY, THE WONDER RABBIT

Magicians love using rabbits in their acts. But some rabbits are fun tricksters themselves! You can astonish your friends with this card trick using a tricky stuffed bunny.

WHAT YOU NEED:

→ A deck of cards
→ A stuffed toy rabbit

PREPARATION:

1. Place all the red cards on the bottom of the deck and all the black cards on the top. When fanned out, the black cards and red cards should be grouped together as shown.

PERFORMANCE:

2. Start by introducing Ricky the Wonder Rabbit to your audience. Say, "Ricky can find a secret hidden card with his amazing sense of smell!"

3. Next, fan out the top half of the deck as shown. Make sure that only the black cards are fanned out. Then ask a volunteer to choose a card and show it to the audience, but not to you or Ricky the Rabbit. This should be one of the black cards.

4. While the volunteer shows the card to the audience, fan the deck as shown so only the red cards are fanned out. Then ask the volunteer to slide the chosen card back into the fanned part of the deck.

5. Now the black card should be mixed in with the red cards and very easy to find. This is the secret of the trick.

TURN PAGE FOR MORE!

6. Now fan out the deck so only you can see the cards. Take the chosen black card from the deck and lay it face down on the table. Tell the volunteer, "I'm not sure, but I think your card could be this one." Be sure to remember where this card is on the table.

7. Take five more cards and lay them on the table in the same way. There will be a total of six cards on the table. Each time you pick a card, tell the volunteer you think it could be the chosen card, but you aren't sure. Be sure to remember where the correct card is.

magic tip: You can make this trick really fun by pretending to scold Ricky for fooling you with his trickery!

8. Now it's time for Ricky the Wonder Rabbit to do his famous trick. Have some fun by handling the rabbit like a puppet. Have Ricky sniff a card. He'll shake his head "no." Flip over the card to show it's not the volunteer's chosen card.

9. Keep playing with Ricky like he's real. Have Ricky sniff at each card and shake his head "no" until there are just two cards left. Make sure one of the leftover cards is the correct one.

10. Now say, "Okay Ricky, there are only two cards left. This is your last chance." Have Ricky sniff at the correct card. Ricky should go wild – bouncing and jumping around. Finally, he'll land on the correct card. Flip over the chosen card and show it to the audience. Have Ricky take a bow as they applaud!

INCREDIBLE MAGIC!

Magicians are storytellers. They weave wild tales about strange places and mysterious people while they perform their fantastic tricks. Now that you've learned some of the basic secrets of magic, you can start adding your own clever stories. It's a great way to keep your audience entertained, and it keeps them from watching your hands too closely.

A MAGIC SECRET - THE DITCH

The Ditch, or secret drop, is one of the most valuable secrets in magic. The audience thinks you're grabbing your magic wand. But at the same time, you secretly drop a hidden object into your magic box. Don't look stiff or nervous while you do this. Just act calm while you smoothly make the switch. The audience won't suspect a thing!

22

THE MAGIC HANKY

Lots of people carry hankies in case they have to sneeze. Where do you think magicians keep their hankies? With this fun trick, you can make a colorful hanky appear from an empty paper bag!

WHAT YOU NEED:

→ A colorful handkerchief
→ Two small paper bags
→ Colorful confetti

PREPARATION:

1. For this trick, you'll need a secret pocket in the bottom of a paper bag. To make it, cut the top half off of one paper bag. Keep the bottom half and set it to the side.

2. Next, place the hanky at the bottom of the second bag. Then place the half bag inside the whole bag on top of the hanky. The hanky is now hidden inside the secret pocket. Now it's time to trick the audience!

3. First, tell the audience about your magic confetti that can create a new hanky any time you need one. Next, pick up the bag and show the audience that it's empty by turning it upside down. Ask a volunteer to stick a hand in the bag to make sure it's empty.

4. Now toss some of the colorful confetti into the bag. Wave your wand over the bag and say a few magic words.

Next, blow the bag up like a balloon. Then twist the top and pop it so the confetti flies out as shown.

5. After startling the audience with the loud bang, it's time to amaze them by pulling out the colorful hanky. Say something like, "Magic confetti is great. It works every time!"

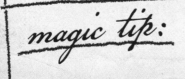 *magic tip:* If you have a rainbow-colored hanky, have the audience pretend to take a tiny pinch of color off their shirts and toss it toward the bag. Then a rainbow-colored hanky amazingly appears!

23

SUNDAY COMICS HERO

People love reading the Sunday comic pages. Everybody has a favorite character. You can make your favorite character appear out of nowhere with this fun trick!

WHAT YOU NEED:

→ Color comics from a
   Sunday newspaper
→ A small toy figure
→ Glue

PREPARATION:

1. First, glue the comics together to make a secret pocket as shown.

2. Then hide the small toy figure inside the secret pocket. A thin, flat toy works best so the audience doesn't see that something is hidden inside.

3. First, hold up the Sunday comics and show them to the audience. Tell them a story about your favorite character. Mention how you love the character's adventures or how the character always makes you laugh. Be sure to keep the secret pocket hidden.

4. Tell the audience that the character sometimes likes to come out and say, "Hello." Then roll the paper into a cone shape so the secret pocket is in the middle. Next, wave your magic wand over the cone and say a few magic words.

5. Finally, reach into the cone and pull out the toy figure. Have the toy take a bow as the audience gives you a round of applause!

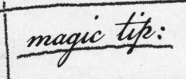

magic tip: You can do this trick with a comic book too. Make a secret pocket by gluing a second back cover onto a comic book. Then just roll the comic book into a tube and let the toy slide out into your hand.

24

MAGIC MAG-NEE-TO MAN

Astonish your friends with your magical magnetic powers! Become the Magical Mag-Nee-To Man and make a plastic cup stick like a magnet to a book. It's an easy gravity-defying trick.

WHAT YOU NEED:

→ A plastic cup
→ A book
→ A paper clip

PREPARATION:

1. First, bend one end of the paper clip so it sticks straight out. Then hold it against the book with your thumb as shown.

2. Now place the cup over the paper clip and press it against the paper clip with your thumb. This is the secret of the trick. With enough practice, you'll be able to hold the book at any angle and the cup should stay in place.

3. First, rub the cup against your hair. While you do this say, "People tell me I have a magnetic personality. And they're right. I can affect objects with my magnetic power!"

4. Now get the book and paper clip from your magic box. Hold up the book and show it to the audience. Be sure they can't see that you are holding the paper clip behind the book. Then place the cup over the paper clip as shown.

5. Firmly hold the cup against the book like you practiced earlier. Then slowly turn the book over to show that the cup is stuck to it. Take a bow as the audience applauds your incredible magnetic abilities!

 Try ending the trick by pretending that the cup is stuck to the book so well that you can't get it off. This will add some fun comedy for the audience.

25

THE ESCAPING COIN

Big or small, all magic tricks are just illusions. Sometimes the best illusions are when the magic happens right in a person's hand. This one will leave the whole audience baffled!

WHAT YOU NEED:

→ Seven pennies

PERFORMANCE:

1. First, tell the audience that money sometimes has a mind of its own and likes to escape. Pick up the pennies one at a time and place them in your left hand. Count them out loud so the audience knows how many there are.

2. Now ask a volunteer to hold out his or her hand. Count out loud as you transfer the coins, one at a time, from your hand into the volunteer's hand.

3. When you get to the sixth penny, tap it against the coins in the volunteer's hand as shown. The sound will cause the volunteer and the audience to believe that it landed with the other coins.

4. Instead of giving the volunteer the sixth penny, simply keep it hidden in your right hand. This will take practice so the volunteer doesn't see that you keep it. Now drop the last penny into the volunteer's hand as shown. Ask your volunteer to close his or her hand tightly so no coins can escape.

Hidden coin

5. Put your hand hiding the secret penny under the volunteer's hand in a fist as shown. Bump the volunteer's hand a couple of times, then let the hidden coin drop into your left hand as shown. Finally, ask the volunteer to count out the number of coins he or she has in their hand. When the volunteer counts only six coins, the audience will think the coin escaped right through your volunteer's closed hand!

26

THE ZOOMING MOON ROCK

Even rocks can get homesick. Here's a trick you can use to send a lonely moon rock zooming back home to the moon. Everybody will be left wondering how it's done!

WHAT YOU NEED:

> → A small, shiny rock
> → Two foam cups
> → A scissors

PREPARATION:

1. First, make a secret hole by cutting out the bottom of one foam cup with the scissors as shown.

2. Next, stack the cups so the cup with the secret hole is on the bottom. Then put the rock in the top cup as shown.

3. First, ask a volunteer in the audience to help you with this trick. Dump the moon rock into the volunteer's hand and ask him or her to show it to the audience. Then tell the audience a story about magical moon rocks that fly home to the moon when they get lonely.

4. Now separate the cups. Be sure to hide the secret hole by keeping that cup in the palm of your hand as shown. Tell the au_____ you're going to se_____ home with some h_____ ur volunteer. Then h_____ lunteer put the rock _____ normal cup.

Secret hole

5. Next, place the two cups together mouth to mouth as shown.

TURN PAGE FOR MORE!

6. Tip over the cups so the rock falls through the secret hole and into your hand as shown. Be sure to keep the hole covered with your hand so the audience won't see it.

7. Next, set the cups on the table so they are stacked mouth to mouth as shown. Be sure to keep the rock hidden in your hand.

Hidden rock

8. Now get your magic wand out of your magic box. As you reach into the box, leave the rock behind as shown.

9. Here's where the magic happens! Wave your magic wand over the stacked cups. You can ask your volunteer to repeat some magic words to help send the rock home too. Then pretend to watch the rock zoom home to the moon.

10. Finally, slam your hand down on the stacked cups to smash them up. Tear up the pieces to show that the rock has disappeared into outer space! Thank the volunteer and ask your audience to give him or her a round of applause!

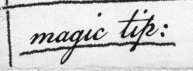

magic tip: Try having the volunteer wave the magic wand over the cups. He or she will be astounded that the rock disappeared!

27

THE TRICKY LEPRECHAUN

Leprechauns are real pranksters. The audience will be amaze[d] when an invisible leprechaun steals a coin. Then they'll have [a] good laugh when you find it hiding in your shoe!

WHAT YOU NEED:

→ Two identical coins
→ A colorful handkerchief
→ A shirt with a chest pocket
→ A tissue

PREPARATION:

1. First, place the tissue [in] the bottom of your shir[t] pocket as shown. This h[elps] keep it open a bit. The[n put] one of the coins in your [...]

PERFORMANCE:

2. Start by telling the audience a story about a tricky, invisible leprechaun that likes to steal coins and hide them. Then hold up the second coin in your left hand and show it to the audience. Hold the hanky in your right hand.

3. Now drag the hanky over your hand and the coin. As you do this, take the coin in your right hand as shown. Be sure to keep the coin behind the hanky so the audience can't see it.

ou drag the hanky
you, secretly drop the
o your shirt pocket as
Keep looking at your
hand under the hanky
udience doesn't
anything.

the coin is hidden, pull
e hanky to show that the
disappeared! Act surprised
ast that tricky Leprechaun
start searching for the coin.
to check your pockets and
magic box. Finally, take off
holding the secret coin.
ience will be amazed that
echaun hid the coin there!

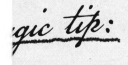 *gic tip:*

Try hiding the secret coin under a chair in the audience instead of inside your shoe. When the coin disappears, ask them to look for it under their chairs. When someone finds it, they can keep it as a gift!

28

MULTIPLYING MONEY

Everybody likes having plenty of money. Magic with money really grabs people's attention. This trick will make the audience wish their money could multiply this fast!

WHAT YOU NEED:

→ Six coins
→ Two popsicle sticks
→ Tape
→ A table and chair

PREPARATION:

1. First, create a secret pocket by taping the popsicle sticks to the bottom of the table as shown. The space between them should be a little smaller than the coins are wide. Be sure the pocket is near the side of the table you'll be sitting at.

2. Next, slide one or two coins into the secret pocket made by the popsicle sticks. The gap between the sticks should allow you to easily get at the coins.

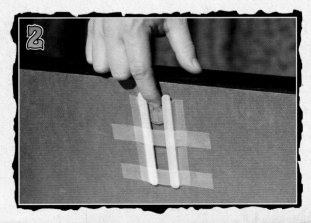

3. Start by laying out the rest of the coins on the table. Tell your audience, "Making money is easy. I can make these coins multiply." Ask a volunteer to count the coins on the table.

...w slide the coins off the edge ... table with one hand so they ...into your other hand.

5. At the same time, use your second hand to slide a coin out of the secret pocket as shown.

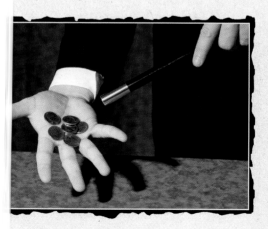

6. Close your hand around the coins, then wave your magic wand over your hand in a mystical way and say a few magic words. Finally, open your hand and have the volunteer recount the coins. The audience will be stunned when they see that the coins have multiplied!

75

29

THE MYSTIC SNOWFLAKE

No two snowflakes are exactly alike. With this trick you can make a paper snowflake with special magical scissors. The audience won't believe their eyes when it magically appears!

WHAT YOU NEED:

→ A scissors
→ Two sheets of paper

PREPARATION:

1. First, fold one sheet of paper in half three or four times. Then cut a few pieces out around the edges as shown to make a paper snowflake.

PERFORMANCE:

2. Leave the paper snowflake folded up. When you're ready to do the trick, take the plain paper out of your magic box. At the same time, hide the paper snowflake in your hand as shown.

Snowflake

3. Tell the audience you can make a snowflake with magic invisible scissors. Show them the plain paper and fold it three or four times. With the final fold, secretly switch the plain paper with the snowflake. Hide the plain paper in the palm of your hand. Be sure the audience doesn't see you switch the two pieces of paper.

Snowflake →

← Hidden paper

Next, use the hand that is hiding plain paper to reach into your pocket for your magic invisible scissors. Leave the paper behind in pocket.

5. Now pretend to pull out the magic invisible scissors. Use your fingers like scissors as shown, and pretend to cut out a paper snowflake.

6. Finally, unfold the paper snowflake and show it to the audience. They will be amazed when they see that the paper has been transformed right before their eyes!

30

THE CRAZY COMICAL SOCK

The best way to warm up an audience is to get them laughing. With this trick, the audience gets a good laugh when you find something you didn't even know was lost!

WHAT YOU NEED:

→ Two identical socks
→ A piece of black cloth
→ A black hat
→ Four safety pins

PREPARATION:

1. First, pin the black cloth into the bottom of the hat to create a secret pocket as shown. Then tuck a sock into the secret pocket.

2. Next, put the other sock on your right foot. Leave your left foot bare under your shoe as shown.

3. Start by telling the audience that you often find the strangest things in your hat. Say, "I never know what I might get when I do this trick." Then hold the hat up to show the audience that it's empty.

4. Now wave your magic wand over the hat and say a few mysterious magic words.

5. Reach into the hat and pull out the sock. Make a funny, confused look on your face. The audience will think something went wrong.

6. While looking confused, lift your right pant leg to show the matching sock. Then quickly lift your left pant leg to show that the sock is missing. Act surprised or embarrassed — as if you made the sock appear in the hat by mistake. The audience will have a good laugh and enjoy the rest of the show!

31

THE MAGIC PENNY BANK

Do you like saving your pennies? Now you can save money in a bottle without even removing the top. Your audience wi be astounded when a coin seems to appear out of nowhere!

WHAT YOU NEED:

→ A plastic juice bottle
→ 3 pennies with the same date
→ A colorful handkerchief
→ Tape

1

PREPARATION:

1. First, place a small loop o tape inside the bottle's cap. Then lightly place one of th pennies on the tape as sho Don't press down too hard the penny or the trick won' work at the end.

2. Ask an adult to help you with this next step. Hide a secret, second penny inside a secret pocket in the hanky. Do this by folding the corner of the hanky over the penny and sewing it in place as shown.

3. First, pick up the bottle and show the audience that it's empty. Tell them that you like to save your extra coins, but that you hate having to open the top all the time. Then gently screw on the top. Be sure the hidden penny doesn't fall into the bottle.

4. Put the bottle down and pick up the third penny. Say, "I like saving my coins by magic instead." Then pretend to place the penny in the center of the hanky. Instead of the third penny, you will really hold the secret penny hidden inside the hanky as shown. Hide the third penny in the palm of your hand.

Secret penny

5. Now ask a volunteer to hold the penny in the hanky. He or she will actually hold the secret penny hidden in the hanky. Be sure to keep the third penny hidden.

TURN PAGE
FOR MORE!

6. Get your magic wand out of your magic box. Drop the hidden third penny into the box as you pick up the wand as shown.

7. Next, wave your magic wand over the hanky and say a few magic words. Then quickly pull the hanky out of the volunteer's hand to show that the penny has vanished!

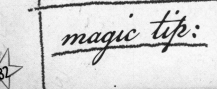

magic tip:

Think of a story to go along with this trick to make it more mysterious and entertaining. Maybe President Lincoln has magical jumping powers. Or maybe the bank belongs to a ghost!

8. Now pick up the bottle and cover it with the hanky. Give the magic wand to the volunteer and ask him or her to wave it over the bottle and say a few magic words. Then tap the bottle firmly against your hand. This should release the secret penny inside the bottle cap so it drops into the bottle. You should hear it rattle inside the bottle.

9. Finally, remove the hanky, open the bottle, and drop the penny into your volunteer's hand. The audience will be amazed at how the coin disappeared from the volunteer's hand and reappeared inside the bottle. Thank the volunteer for helping and ask the audience to give him or her a round of applause!

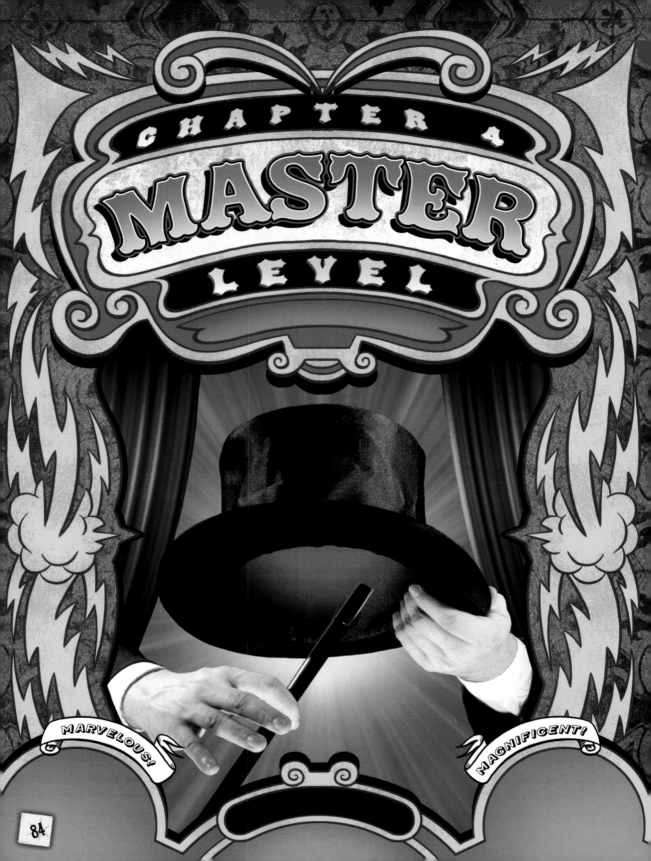

FANTASTIC MAGIC!

You've learned how to make things appear and disappear. You've learned how to read people's minds. And you've learned how to entertain your audience. Now it's time to learn some more complicated tricks. When you put all these things together, people will believe you're a master magician! Remember, magicians always make sure their audience enjoys the show — and they never give away their secrets!

A MAGIC SECRET - MISDIRECTION

Misdirection is an important part of magic. People tend to follow a magician's gaze to whatever he or she looks at. Magicians misdirect audiences by focusing their eyes on what they want people to see. Then they can secretly hide an object while the audience's attention is on something else. With enough practice, you can become a master of misdirection too!

32

THE IMPOSSIBLE COIN

Magicians have been doing coin tricks for thousands of years. This trick will really stump your audience. People won't believe their eyes when a coin disappears into thin air!

WHAT YOU NEED:

→ One playing card
→ Two identical coins
→ Glue

PREPARATION:

1. First, glue one coin to the face side of the playing card as shown. Then put the other coin into your pocket.

PERFORMANCE:

2. Begin by telling the audience how tricky money can be. Say, "Sometimes coins disappear right out of my hand!" Then show them the card with the coin. Be sure not to tip it, or they will see that the coin is stuck to the card.

3. Next, turn the card toward you as shown and pretend to dump the coin into your hand. Turning the card toward you keeps people from seeing that the coin is stuck to the card.

4. Now close your hand and pretend to hold the coin. Then toss the card into your magic box and pick up your magic wand.

5. Tap your hand with the wand three times. Then open your hand to show the coin has vanished.

6. Finally, reach into your pocket and bring out the second coin. The audience will believe it's the same coin that just vanished. They'll really wonder how the coin jumped from your hand into your pocket!

33

THE TRICKY LIZARD

Most reptiles aren't very fast. But this tricky lizard can zip out of sight in a split second. Your audience will have a good laugh when they see it climbing on your back!

WHAT YOU NEED:

→ A large piece of cardboard
→ A small toy lizard
→ Black thread
→ A safety pin
→ A black shirt or jacket

PREPARATION:

Pin

1. First, draw a desert scene on the cardboard with lots of cactuses, sand, and tumbleweeds. Next, tie one end of the thread to the safety pin and the other end to the toy lizard. Then attach the pin to the back of your shirt or jacket collar as shown.

2. Next, bring the toy lizard under your arm so the thread runs under it as shown. Then place the lizard in your chest pocket. The audience should not be able to see the thread when it's hidden against the black shirt or jacket.

Thread

3. Pull the toy lizard out of your pocket and show it to the audience. Tell them a story about how hard it is to keep track of the tricky reptile. Let them know it often disappears and tries to get back to its desert home.

4. Next, cover the lizard with the desert picture as shown. As you do this, secretly drop the lizard and let it swing around to land on your back. Then pull away the picture to show that the lizard has vanished!

5. Now pretend to look around for the tricky lizard. Where did it go? Ask the audience if they saw where it went. Finally, turn around. The audience will see the lizard hanging on your back. Act amazed and confused about how it got there. The audience will get a big laugh out of this trick!

34

THE MAGIC ACE

The Ace of Spades is the world's most magical card. This trick will blow your friends away when the ace turns invisible and magically appears in your pocket!

WHAT YOU NEED:

→ Two identical Ace of Spades
→ Seven other cards, any color
→ Glue
→ Scissors
→ A table

PREPARATION:

1. First put one Ace of Spades in your pocket. Then cut the other ace in half diagonally and glue one half to another card as shown.

2. The secret to this trick is in how you hold the cards. The Ace of Spades can be seen when the cards are fanned out one way. But when the cards are turned around and fanned out again, the ace is hidden.

3. First, tell the audience a story about the magical ace. Say, "The Ace of Spades can turn invisible any time it wants." Next, fan the cards out so the audience can see the ace. Ask someone if they can see the Ace of Spades. Then turn the cards over and pretend to take out an invisible card as shown.

4. Next, put down the cards and pretend to put the invisible ace in your pocket. Then, pick up the cards again. As you pick them up, be sure to turn the cards around. Keep talking to the audience as you do this so they don't notice that you turn the cards around. Now fan out the cards again and show the audience that the Ace of Spades has disappeared!

5. Finally, reach into your pocket and pull out the secret Ace of Spades. Show it to your audience. Ask them to give the ace a round of applause as you pretend that it takes a bow!

35

TOMMY, THE TRAINED PING-PONG BALL

Normal ping-pong balls just bounce around a lot. But this magic ping-pong ball can do a great trick. People will be astonished when it does an amazing balancing act!

WHAT YOU NEED:

→ A ping-pong ball
→ A magic wand
→ Black thread
→ Tape
→ Scissors

PREPARATION:

1. First, cut a piece of thread a little longer than the magic wand. Then use small pieces of tape to attach the thread to the wand on both ends. Make sure the thread stays a little loose in the middle.

PERFORMANCE:

2. Start by bouncing the ping-pong ball on the table a couple of times. Tell the audience a story about the ball. Say, "Tommy looks like a normal ping-pong ball. But he is really a magic ball. He can do a fun balancing act!"

3. When you're ready to do the trick, hold the wand with your thumbs under the thread as shown. The thread will help balance the ball.

4. Be sure to keep the thread facing you so the audience can't see it. Now place the ball on the wand and balance it on the thread.

5. To the audience, the ball will look like it is balancing on the wand. Gently tilt the wand up and down a little so the ball travels back and forth. The ball will seem to be doing a dangerous balancing act.

To end the trick, toss the ball up in the air, catch it, and toss it to someone in the audience. While they look at it, toss the wand into your magic box. Then ask the audience for a round of applause for the tricky ball!

36

THE NUMBER ONE FAN

This trick will astound any sports fan. Your audience will be stunned when you pull a big-league sports star out of a hat!

WHAT YOU NEED:

→ A giant foam finger
→ A baseball hat
→ 2 identical sports cards
→ 5 other sports cards
→ Tape

PREPARATION:

1. First, place a circle of tape on the back of one of the identical cards. Then tuck the secret card into the baseball hat along one side as shown. Be sure the tape faces the inside of the hat and isn't stuck on anything.

PERFORMANCE:

2. Begin by asking if there are any sports fans in the audience. Then bring out the cards and name off the players. Lay the cards on the table as shown. Make sure the second identical card is the third card in from your left. Next, ask someone to choose a number between one and six.

Forced card

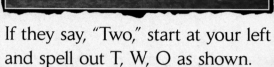

If they say, "One," start at your left and spell out O, N, E as shown.

If they say, "Two," start at your left and spell out T, W, O as shown.

If they say, "Three," start at your left and count 1, 2, 3 as shown.

If they say, "Four," start from your right and count 1, 2, 3, 4 as shown.

If they say, "Five," start at your right again and spell out F, I, V, E as shown.

If they say, "Six," start at your left and spell S, I, X as shown.

TURN PAGE FOR MORE!

Secret card

3. When you land on the forced card, hold it up and tell the audience which one it is. Now show them your magic foam finger. Say, "This magic finger can help me find the chosen card." Next, hold up the hat to show that it's empty. Be sure to cover the secret card with your hand as shown so the audience can't see it.

4. Now toss all the cards into the hat and shake them up a little. Don't shake too hard or the secret card might fall in with the rest of the cards. The rest of the trick will be ruined if this happens.

magic tip: When you count out the cards based on a chosen number, you will always land on the card you want. This is called "forcing" a card.

5. Next, put on the magic foam finger and dip it into the hat as shown. Make it fun for the audience by pretending to dig around inside the hat a little. You can even pretend that the finger gets stuck on something. When you're ready for the big finish, press the finger against the tape on the secret card so it sticks to the end.

6. Finally, slowly pull the foam finger out of the hat. Show the audience that the chosen card is magically stuck on the end. Say, "The magic finger never fails to find the card!" Then take a bow as the audience applauds!

37

THE COIN MULTIPLYING BOOK

Sometimes coins are found in the strangest places. This trick will stun your audience when a magic book instantly multiplies the coins in a volunteer's hands.

WHAT YOU NEED:

> Eight coins
> An old book
> Scissors
> Glue

PREPARATION:

1. First, make a secret pocket in the old book. Cut out a small space at the bottom of the book as shown. Make sure the pocket is big enough to fit two coins inside. Don't make it too big or the audience might see the hole.

2. Next, glue the pages together around the secret pocket as shown. When the glue is dry, place two coins in the secret pocket.

3. Tell the audience about your special magic book. Say, "This magic book can instantly make coins multiply." Then place six coins on top of the book. Ask a volunteer to help you with this trick. Ask the volunteer to count the coins out loud. Then quickly tip the book so all the coins, including the hidden ones, slide into the volunteer's hand.

4. Tell the volunteer to hold the coins tightly in his or her hand. Then lightly tap the book two times on top of the volunteer's hand. Ask, "Did you feel anything happen inside your hand?" The volunteer will probably say they didn't feel anything at all.

5. Finally, ask the volunteer to put the coins on the table and count them out loud again. The audience will be amazed when they see there are now eight coins. Thank the volunteer and ask the audience to give him or her a round of applause!

magic tip: Always keep the secret pocket facing you so the audience and volunteer can't see the hole with the hidden coins.

38

THE SPOOKY SPOON

Even ghosts like going on picnics. Your friends will be spooked when this ghostly spoon disappears right before their eyes! With practice, you can make this simple trick look awesome!

WHAT YOU NEED:

- A plastic spoon
- About 2 feet (0.6 meter) of thin elastic
- A safety pin
- A jacket with long sleeves
- An electric drill

PREPARATION:

1. First, ask an adult to drill a small hole in the end of the spoon handle as shown. Then tie one end of the elastic through the hole in the spoon and the other end to the safety pin.

2. Next, connect the safety pin to the inside of your jacket at the shoulder. Then run the spoon and elastic down the inside of the jacket sleeve as shown.

3. Just before you do this trick, step off the stage or behind the curtain so the audience can't see you. Pull the spoon out of your sleeve and hold it in your hand as shown. Then tell the audience a story about the ghostly spoon. Say, "This spooky spoon belongs to a ghost. Sometimes it takes the spoon back without any warning!"

4. Now cover the spoon with both hands. Begin rubbing your hands together in a mysterious way.

5. When you cover the spoon, let it go so the elastic can pull it back up your sleeve as shown.

6. Finally, open your hands and show the audience that the spoon has vanished into thin air. Say, "I guess the ghost was ready for his dinner and wanted his spoon back!"

39

THE MAGIC MATCHBOX BANK

You can save money without making a trip to the bank! Just sprinkle some magic dust and your coins travel to a safe place. This magical traveling penny will keep your audience in awe.

WHAT YOU NEED:

→ Two pennies with the same date
→ An empty matchbox

PREPARATION:

1. Place one of the pennies between the inner and outer parts of the matchbox as shown. Make sure the penny is completely covered so the audience won't see it.

PERFORMANCE:

2. First, show the audience that the matchbox is empty. Say, "I've found a new kind of savings bank." Then close the box so the secret penny slides into it, and set it aside. Next, take out the second penny and ask a volunteer to read the date.

Hidden penny

3. Take back the penny and hold it between your thumb and first finger. Then pretend to grab the penny with your other hand. Instead of grabbing it, you will drop it into your palm as shown. It looks like you're holding the coin in the second hand, but you are really hiding it in the palm of the first hand. This old trick is called the French Drop.

4. Now reach into your pocket for some magic dust. Leave the hidden penny in your pocket, then sprinkle magic dust over your empty hand.

5. Next, open your hands wide to show the audience that the penny has vanished!

6. Finally, open the matchbox and take out the secret penny. Show it to the audience and ask the volunteer to read the date again. They will be stunned at how the penny magically traveled from your hand to the matchbox!

40

THE EGG-STRAORDINARY EGG

Are you ever in a hurry and don't have time for lunch? With this fun trick you can make an egg magically appear and cook it up fast. You'll leave the audience wondering how it's done!

WHAT YOU NEED:

→ A hat
→ A handkerchief
→ A plastic egg
→ A plastic "cooked" egg
→ A plate
→ Thread
→ A needle

PREPARATION:

1. Ask an adult to help you prepare this trick. First, poke two small holes in one end of the plastic egg with the needle. Then slide the thread through the holes and tie it to the egg as shown. Make sure the thread is the same color as your hanky.

2. Next, sew the other end of the thread to the hanky. The plastic egg should be about 1 inch (2.5 centimeters) from the edge of the hanky as shown. Finally, put the plastic "cooked" egg into the hat.

"Cooked" egg

3. First, tell the audience that you're feeling hungry. Say, "I think it's time for a snack." Then pick up the hat and show the audience that it's empty. When you pick it up, hide the "cooked" egg under your hand as shown. Then put the hat down and let the "cooked" egg drop into it.

4. Next, pick up the hanky by the corners as shown so the egg hangs behind the hanky. Be sure to do this with the egg facing you so the audience can't see it.

5. Now fold the hanky in half with the egg inside. Hold it above the hat and say, "Cluck, Cluck, Cluck!" Then let the egg fall from the hanky into the hat as shown.

6. Next, quickly drag the hanky over the hat. Then raise it up so the egg is lifted out of the hat and hidden like before. Toss the hanky and egg into your magic box. Now pick up the hat and pretend to "cook" the egg inside by blowing on it. Finally, flip the hat over the plate and show the audience your delicious cooked egg!

41

THE AMAZING HEALING ROPE

Your audience will have a great time with this funny rope trick. They'll think you goofed at first. But they'll be stunned when the rope is magically healed right before their eyes!

WHAT YOU NEED:

- Two pieces of rope about 3 feet (1 meter) long
- Two pieces of rope about 4 inches (10 centimeters) long
- Two large paper bags
- Scissors
- Tape

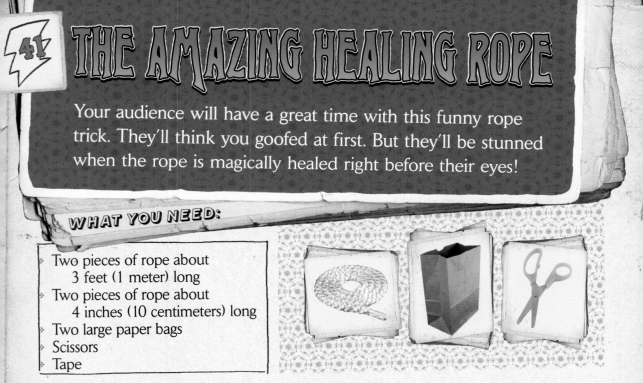

PREPARATION:

1. First, cut one of the paper bags in half lengthwise as shown.

2. Then tape the half bag inside the whole bag to make a secret pocket as shown.

3. Next, make a small loop about 1 foot (0.3 meter) from the end of one of the long ropes. Then tie a loose knot around the loop with one of the short rope pieces as shown above. The long rope should look like it has been cut and tied back together.

4. Now tie another knot in the same way about 1 foot (0.3 meter) from the other end of the long rope. The rope should now look similar to the picture.

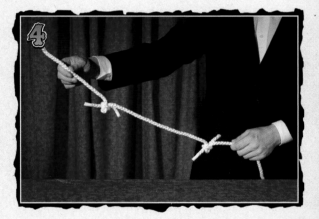

5. Place the knotted rope into the paper bag. Leave the secret pocket empty.

TURN PAGE FOR MORE!

6. First, tell the audience that you have a trick that will astound them. Then show them the second long rope and say, "This amazing magic rope can heal itself if it's cut." Then hold up the rope and cut it into three equal pieces.

7. Next, slide the three pieces of rope into the secret pocket in the paper bag. Don't let the audience see the secret pocket!

8. Now shake the bag around a little. Pretend that the pieces of rope are jumping around inside and are trying to heal themselves. You can also wave your magic wand over the bag as you do this.

9. Next, reach into the bag and pull out the knotted rope. Toss the bag out of sight. Say, "The rope is whole again! Isn't that amazing?" The audience will probably laugh when they see that the rope is just tied together. Try acting confused. But tell them that you can fix it. You just need a volunteer's help. Ask someone to help you fix the rope.

10. Ask the volunteer to blow on one of the knots. As he or she blows, pull the rope tight as shown. The knot should pop right off the rope. Say, "Wow! You're better at this than I thought!"

11. Finally, ask the volunteer to blow on the other knot. Pull the rope tight so the other knot pops off like before. Show the magically healed rope to the audience. Thank the volunteer and ask him or her to take a bow while the audience gives you both a round of applause!

INDEX

Edge Books are published by Capstone Press.
151 Good Counsel Drive, P.O. Box 669, Mankato, Minnesota 56002.
www.capstonepress.com

Library of Congress Cataloging-in-Publication Data
Barnhart, Norm.
    Amazing magic tricks / by Norm Barnhart.
    Includes index.
    Summary: "Step-by-step instructions and clear photos describe how to
perform a variety of magic tricks at different levels" — Provided by publisher.
    ISBN-13: 978-1-4296-2916-4 (paperback)
    ISBN-10: 1-4296-2916-9 (paperback)
    1. Magic tricks — Juvenile literature. I. Title. II. Series.
GV1548.B36 2009
793.8 — dc22   2008002575

Editorial Credits
Aaron Sautter, editor; Kyle Grenz, book designer; Bob Lentz, designer/illustrator;
    Marcy Morin, scheduler

Photo Credits
Capstone Press/Karon Dubke, cover and interior photos
Shutterstock, 89 (desert scene); Chen Ping Hung; javarman; Marilyn Volan;
    Tatiana53; Tischenko Irina, backgrounds

1 2 3 4 5 6 13 12 11 10 09 08